CELEBRITY BIOS

Lauryn Hill

by
Cynthia Laslo

HIGH
interest
books

Children's Books
A Division of Grolier Publishing
New York / London / Hong Kong / Sydney
Danbury, Connecticut

Photo Credits: Cover, p. 11 (both) © Everett collection; pp. 4, 18, 27 © Fitzroy Barrett/Globe Photos Inc.; p. 12 © Anders Krusberg/Globe Photos Inc.; p. 16, © Neal Preston/Globe Photos Inc.; pp. 21, 30 © Henry McGee/Globe Photos Inc.; p. 22 © Ashley Knoter/Alpha/Globe Photos; p.28 © Lisa Rose/Globe Photos; p. 32 © Dave Benett/Alpha/Globe Photos; p. 37 © Walter Weissman/Globe Photos.

Visit Children's Press on the Internet at:
http://publishing.grolier.com

Library of Congress Cataloging-in-Publication Data

Laslo, Cynthia, 1943-
  Lauryn Hill / by Cynthia Laslo.
    p. cm.—(Celebrity bios)
  Summary: A biography of the young African American singer from New Jersey who won five Grammy awards in 1999, including Best New Artist.
    ISBN 0-516-23322-x (lib. bdg.)—ISBN 0-516-23522-2 (pbk.)
    1. Hill, Lauryn—Juvenile literature. 2. Singers—United States Biography—Juvenile literature. [1. Hill, Lauryn. 2. Singers. 3. Women—Biography. 4. Afro-Americans—Biography.] I. Title. II. Series.

ML3930.H55 L37 2000
782.421649'092—dc21
[B]
                                                                99-044798

CONTENTS

CHAPTER ONE

Determination

I was just a little girl
Skinny legs, a press and curl
My mother always thought I'd be a star . . .
—"Every Ghetto, Every City" from
The Miseducation of Lauryn Hill

February 24, 1999. At the Shrine Auditorium in Los Angeles, the 41st Annual Grammy Awards are taking place. Tonight, one woman is nominated for ten Grammy Awards. At the end of the evening she takes home five Grammys—setting a record for the most awarded to any female artist.

Lauryn Hill has won more Grammy Awards than any other female artist.

The woman is Lauryn Hill, and the record that won all of those Grammys was *The Miseducation of Lauryn Hill*. The album was about Lauryn's life and her opinions, her past and her future. "The album is more for me than it is for anyone else," Hill told *Launch online*. "To me these songs were a way for me to express myself and finally just move on. It's like once you're in a storm, it's not until you drive past [it] that you can look back and say, 'Oh my god, that's where I just came from.'"

EARLY DAYS

Lauryn was born on May 26, 1975, in South Orange, New Jersey, a town about 25 miles from New York City. Her parents are Valerie, a junior high school teacher, and Mal, a computer expert.

Music always played a large role in the Hill family. Lauryn's mom played piano, her dad sang at nightclubs and weddings, and her older brother, Malaney, played guitar, drums, and saxophone. It was only a matter of time before Lauryn's musical talents became clear.

As a toddler, Lauryn loved to sing in front of the bathroom mirror. When she was a young girl, Lauryn sang in her church choir and in gospel groups with her family. She always had a strong singing voice and enjoyed performing.

Lauryn's parents also had a large collection of classic soul albums with which Lauryn loved to sing along. "There was something sacred about those old records," Lauryn told *Entertainment Weekly.* Albums by '60s and '70s soul artists, such as Gladys Knight, Roberta Flack, and Marvin Gaye, would have a big influence on Lauryn's future music career. Yet Lauryn also admired many of the R&B artists of the 1980s. When the teenage Lauryn tried karaoke at Six Flags theme park, she chose to sing a Whitney Houston song.

A GIFTED PERFORMER

Lauryn's singing career began early—at age thirteen. Lauryn auditioned for Amateur Night on "Showtime at the Apollo," a television program. The Apollo is a famous New York theater featuring African-American performers, and it was a great honor to sing there. Lauryn not only sang, she got a standing ovation after she performed a Smokey Robinson tune, "Who's Lovin' You." It was the beginning of Lauryn's success on the stage.

Around the same time, when Lauryn was a freshman at Columbia High School, she began singing in a rap group. It was a trio, made up of Lauryn (who used the performing name L-Boogie), classmate Prakazrel Michel (Pras), and his cousin, Wyclef Jean (Clef). They called their group Tranzlator Crew, and they played at local talent shows and high schools.

In addition to singing with the group, Lauryn found time to go on auditions. In 1991, fifteen-year-old Lauryn got a part in an Off-Broadway musical called *Club 12*. *Club 12* was a modern version of William Shakespeare's play *Twelfth Night*, set to hip-hop music. Although the show wasn't a success, a talent agent recognized Lauryn's skill as an actress. Soon after, the agent helped Lauryn to win a role on the popular soap opera "As The World Turns." Lauryn played Kira Johnson, an abused teenage runaway.

Did you know?

In junior high, Lauryn sang the national anthem at a school basketball game. People liked her version so much that it was recorded and played at later games.

Then Lauryn moved on to the big screen, with a small part in the 1993 movie *King of the Hill*. That same year, she won a much larger role in the movie *Sister Act 2: Back in the Habit*. The movie starred Whoopi Goldberg, and Lauryn played a troubled high school student. In one scene, Lauryn's character, Rita Watson, starts rapping in front of her classmates. Director Bill Duke recalls in an interview with *Time*, "None of that was scripted. That was all Lauryn. She was amazing."

DOING IT ALL

While Lauryn pursued an acting career, she remained a very involved student. She got straight As throughout high school and took advanced classes. Lauryn also wrote poetry, took dancing and acting classes, started a gospel choir at school, played the violin, was on the basketball team, and ran track. Still, Lauryn found time to rehearse with bandmates Clef and Pras, staying true to her first love—music.

Lauryn played a troubled
schoolgirl and displayed her
singing talents in 1993's
Sister Act 2.

CHAPTER TWO

Scoring with the Fugees

Sometimes it seems
We'll touch that dream
All we need is dedication . . .
— "Everything is Everything" from
The Miseducation of Lauryn Hill

Using the money she earned from acting, Lauryn was able to help buy music equipment for her band. By 1992, the trio, which changed its name from Tranzlator Crew to the Fugees, had been playing together for about three years. The Fugees began to have a lot of fans in New York and New Jersey. Describing what it was like to

Lauryn started singing with the Fugees when she was just a teenager.

Did you know?

Lauryn studied history at Columbia University in New York City. She put college on hold after the success of the Fugees' second album.

play with the group on a school night, Lauryn told *Teen People*, "I remember doing my homework in the bathroom stalls of hip-hop clubs." Finally, in 1992, Ruffhouse/ Columbia Records recognized the group's talent and signed them to a record contract.

Lauryn was only seventeen when the Fugees recorded the album *Blunted on Reality*. When *Blunted on Reality* was released in early 1994, it was not a hit. The Fugees toured the country to support the album. However, their concert appearances were not as successful as they had hoped.

THE FUGEES TAKE OFF

The Fugees did not give up. They took one of the singles from *Blunted on Reality*, "Nappy Heads," and mixed the music and vocals in a different way. This time, Lauryn's singing was highlighted. The new version of the song began to get attention as a single in dance clubs. The group remixed another song, "Vocab," and finally the Fugees' music began to get played on the radio and on MTV. The Fugees also went on a worldwide tour. People began to take notice of the group's unique sound, and especially of the beautiful female singer, Lauryn Hill.

In 1995, the Fugees went back into the recording studio to make another album. This time, they wanted to create more of a hip-hop sound. Lauryn began singing, in addition to rapping, on many of the songs. Lauryn didn't just sing, though. She helped to write and produce the music that the Fugees were recording. She was contributing to the overall sound of the record.

Roberta Flack sings the remake of her hit song
"Killing Me Softly" with Lauryn Hill.

Fellow Fugee Pras once told *Essence* magazine,
"If Lauryn weren't there, the Fugees wouldn't
be what they are now . . . it would've been a
whole different thing."

In 1996, the Fugees released their second
album, *The Score*. The first single off *The Score*

was "Fu-Gee-La," which immediately landed on the Top 40 radio chart. The song that really hit it big, though, was "Killing Me Softly." It was a hip-hop cover of the 1974 song by Roberta Flack. Lauryn sang the lead vocals, and the song became a gigantic hit all over the world. "There's a whole generation who have no idea who Roberta Flack is," Lauryn told *Entertainment Weekly*. They definitely knew about Lauryn Hill, though, and "Killing Me Softly" rocketed to number one on the music charts.

The Score went on to sell more than 17 million copies, making it one of the best-selling rap/hip-hop albums in history. It also won two Grammy awards in 1997—Best Rap Album and Best R&B Performance by a Duo or Group (for "Killing Me Softly"). Lauryn was on her way to making music history.

CHAPTER THREE

Standing Strong

And every time I try to be
What someone has thought of me
So caught up, I wasn't able to achieve
But deep in my heart the answer it was in me
And I made up my mind to find my own destiny.
— "The Miseducation of Lauryn Hill" from
The Miseducation of Lauryn Hill

In 1996, while on tour with the Fugees to support *The Score*, Lauryn fell in love. She met Rohan Marley, one of the sons of Bob Marley, the famous reggae singer. Rohan was also a well-known football star from the University of Miami.

Lauryn with Rohan Marley

Near the end of the tour, twenty-one-year-old Lauryn realized that she was pregnant with Rohan's child.

A DIFFICULT DECISION

Some people told Lauryn that she should not have the baby. They believed it would slow down her career just as it was getting started. Other people thought that, as an unwed mother, Lauryn would be setting a bad example for young people. Lauryn refused to let others influence her decision and chose to have the baby. In the summer of 1997, Lauryn gave birth to her son, Zion David Marley. Explaining her decision to have Zion, Lauryn told *Essence*, "It was very strange to me how it became such an issue . . . but what began as something dark became the brightest and most important thing to me."

Lauryn was raised as a member of the Methodist church. Her strong faith helped her to make the difficult decision. Lauryn's beliefs have

always been very important to her. "Talking about God doesn't embarrass me," she told *People*. "It doesn't make me less cool."

In 1997, Lauryn broke away from the Fugees
to make her own album.

MAKING IT ON HER OWN

Choosing to have a child was not the only hard decision Lauryn had to make that year. *The Score* had been so successful that there was a lot of pressure to record another album with the Fugees. Lauryn had other plans, though. She had a lot of her own ideas about what she wanted to do with her music.

Lauryn was pregnant with Zion when she decided to record an album of her own, called a solo album. The months before her son was born were very busy ones. Lauryn used the time during her pregnancy to focus on her music. She experimented with different instruments in the recording studio to achieve a multicultural sound. She also became inspired during a trip to Jamaica, where she recorded some songs in the same studio that Bob Marley had used.

To write her songs, Lauryn looked to events in her own life for inspiration. "Every time I got hurt, every time I was disappointed, every time

I learned, I just wrote a song," Lauryn explained to *imusic online*. She wrote songs about fame, about past relationships, about her family. The song closest to Lauryn's heart is "To Zion." In it, Lauryn wrote about her determination to give birth to a child, despite many people telling her that she was making the wrong choice.

GETTING IT RIGHT

Because Lauryn's songs were so personal, she was committed to making a record that was true to her experience. She also knew that she was ready for the challenge of making her own album. "I guess people figure [producing] is something that women don't really know about," Lauryn told *Essence*. "But I was already a legitimate producer." As always, Lauryn intended to record the very best album she possibly could. "I'm a perfectionist," she told *imusic online*. "If I have to do it a hundred times, I'll do it a hundred times!"

HITTING THE BIG TIME

The result of all Lauryn's hard work was *The Miseducation of Lauryn Hill*. The album was released in August 1998. It sold more copies in its first week than any other album by a female artist—more than 420,000 copies. The record was a best-seller not only in the United States but also in Japan, Canada, England, and France.

Music critics loved the album. Fans loved it, too. The first single off the album, "Doo Wop (That Thing)" was certified gold in just two months. By December, *The Miseducation of Lauryn Hill* had gone from gold to platinum to triple platinum. As of June 1999, *The Miseducation of Lauryn Hill* has sold more than 10 million copies worldwide.

ARTIST OF THE YEAR

On January 5, 1999, the Grammy nominations were announced in Los Angeles. Lauryn was nominated for ten awards. She eventually took home five of those Grammys: Album of the Year, Best New Artist, Best Female R&B Vocal Performance, Best R&B Song, and Best R&B Album.

That was just the beginning of Lauryn's honors. That same year, at the 13th Annual Soul Train Music Awards, *The Miseducation of Lauryn Hill* won Best R&B/Soul or Rap Album and Best Female R&B/Soul Album. "Doo Wop (That Thing)" picked up Best Female R&B/Soul Single and Best R&B/Soul Music Video. At the 26th Annual American Music Awards, Lauryn won for Favorite New Soul/R&B Artist, and at the 1998 Billboard Music Awards, she won for Best R&B Album.

Additionally, Lauryn won four NAACP Awards in 1999, including Outstanding Female Artist and Best Album. She also was named Entertainer/Artist of the Year by the magazines *Spin*, *Details*, and *Entertainment Weekly*. *Time*, the *New York Times*, *Rolling Stone*, and *USA Today* named *The Miseducation of Lauryn Hill* Best Album of the Year.

Lauryn holding one of her many Soul Train music awards

Lauryn won for Best R&B Album at the 1998 Billboard Music Awards.

USING HER TALENTS

Lauryn has worked with many other artists since releasing her record. She wrote and produced Aretha Franklin's song "A Rose Is Still A Rose" and directed the music video. She produced "On That Day" for the gospel singer Cece Winans. She produced Whitney Houston's hit song "My Love" and wrote and produced a song for Mary J. Blige. She also worked with Latino guitarist Carlos Santana on a track for his newest album, *Supernatural.*

Did you know?

Lauryn was offered a starring role in Oprah Winfrey's 1998 movie *Beloved.* She had to drop out of the project because she was pregnant with her second child.

CHAPTER FOUR

More Than Music

"In my travels all over the world, I have come to realize that what distinguishes one child from another is not ability but access; access to education, access to opportunity, access to love." — Lauryn on The Refugee Project, her nonprofit organization

In 1996, Lauryn founded an organization to help young people called The Refugee Project. The goal of The Refugee Project is to change the lives of young people for the better. It focuses on non-violence, communication, and education. "I started the non-profit organization because everybody

George Michael (left) and Lauryn Hill at a benefit for
The Refugee Project

needs encouragement and inspiration, especially
our youth," Lauryn explained to *Girl*. Lauryn realized that many kids do not have either the family
support or the determination that she had as a

girl. She also knew how hard life can be for youths growing up in the city. Lauryn founded The Refugee Project for these kids. She wanted to give them access to the opportunities they would need to succeed.

Did you know?

Many famous people participate in The Refugee Project, including Busta Rhymes, Mariah Carey, Spike Lee, Nas, Sean "Puffy" Combs, and D'Angelo.

GIVING BACK

The Refugee Project is the charity that is closest to Lauryn's heart, but it is definitely not the only group she supports. In 1996, when *The Score* was climbing the charts, the Fugees organized a free concert in Harlem, a section of New York City. It featured some of the biggest hip-hop artists, including Sean "Puffy" Combs. At the concert, people were encouraged to register to vote. The Fugees also raised money for Haitian refugees and their children in a benefit concert, the first ever staged by an American group. Lauryn also taped an anti-drug public service announcement for the Musician Assistance Program. Her dedication to helping others is an inspiration to many people.

FAMILY LIFE

Lauryn's dedication also extends to her family. Her relationship with Rohan Marley has remained strong, even though they are not married. "We haven't been in front of a minister yet, but we will be soon," Lauryn told *Entertainment Weekly* in late 1998. Their two children, son Zion and daughter Selah Louise, accompany Rohan and Lauryn every-where. Lauryn told *Teen People,* "I'm not, like, a pretend mother. It's very important that I raise [my children] and provide them with the necessary tools to go out there and be healthy, happy people."

Lauryn also likes being near to her family. In 1997, she and Rohan moved into the South Orange, New Jersey, house where she grew up. She bought her parents a new house right down the street. She also bought houses nearby for her brother, Malaney, and for her grandmother.

It may be hard to believe that, with all of her success, Lauryn stays in the same town where she grew up. "The place keeps me very familiar with who I am," Lauryn told *Teen People* about South Orange. "I love my home, I loved growing up there and I will raise my children there." Another reason, Lauryn told *Details*, is that "when it comes to hip-hop, it's very important to stay in touch with who you are, so I probably won't ever move very far away."

THE FUTURE

Lauryn Hill has achieved enormous success as a musician, an actress, a mother, a producer, and an activist. What is next for this talented young

woman? In 1998, Lauryn returned to acting. She
starred in a small, independent film called
Restaurant. The movie hasn't been released in
theaters, but it received good reviews at film festivals. Madonna has asked Lauryn to appear in a
movie being made by her production company,
Mad Guy Films. There is also a possibility that
Lauryn will play Rita Marley, Bob Marley's wife,
in an upcoming biographical film. Lauryn also
has her own production company, and she's inter-
ested in making science-fiction movies.

In April 1999, Lauryn kicked off her world
tour in Japan. It then moved to the United States
and will continue in Africa and Europe. There is
also talk that the Fugees will get back together to
record another album. "Once a Fugee, always a
Fugee," Lauryn told *Time.*

Whatever Lauryn decides to do next, you can be
sure she'll do it her way—with energy, confidence,
and style. As all of her fans know, everything she
does comes straight from the heart!

Lauryn's 1999 tour sold out all over the world.

TIMELINE

1975	• Lauryn Hill is born in South Orange, New Jersey, on May 26.
1988–1989	• Lauryn sings on "Showtime at the Apollo." • Lauryn begins singing in the rap group Tranzlator Crew.
1991	• Lauryn gets a part in the Off-Broadway musical *Club 12*. • Lauryn is cast as Kira Johnson on the soap opera "As the World Turns."
1992	• Tranzlator Crew changes its name to the Fugees and is signed by Ruffhouse/Columbia Records.
1993	• Lauryn is cast in the movie *King of the Hill*. • Lauryn plays a high school student in Whoopi Goldberg's *Sister Act 2: Back in the Habit*.
1994	• The Fugees release their first album, *Blunted on Reality*. • Lauryn attends Columbia University in New York City.
1995–1996	• The Fugees record and release their second album, *The Score*. • Lauryn leaves college to devote time to the Fugees. • The Fugees tour worldwide.

- Lauryn meets Rohan Marley.
- Lauryn founds the nonprofit organization The Refugee Project.
- The Fugees organize a benefit concert in Harlem.

1997
- *The Score* wins two Grammy awards: Best Rap Album and Best R&B Performance by a Duo or Group.
- Lauryn begins recording her solo album.
- Lauryn gives birth to Zion David Marley.
- Lauryn and Rohan move into Lauryn's childhood home in New Jersey.

1998
- *The Miseducation of Lauryn Hill* is released in August.
- The album goes triple platinum by the end of the year.
- The single "Doo Wop (That Thing)" goes gold in two months.
- The independent film *Restaurant*, which stars Lauryn, is shown at several film festivals.
- Lauryn wins Best R&B Album at the Billboard Awards.
- Lauryn collaborates with Aretha Franklin, Cece Winans, Mary J. Blige, and Carlos Santana on their albums.
- Lauryn's daughter, Selah Louise, is born in November.

1999	• Lauryn is nominated for ten Grammy Awards and wins five, including Album of the Year and Best R&B Album.
	• Lauryn wins four Soul Train Music Awards, one American Music Award, and four NAACP Awards.
	• Lauryn begins a sold-out international tour in April.

FACT SHEET

Name	Lauryn Hill
Born	May 26, 1975
Birthplace	South Orange, New Jersey
Mother	Valerie
Father	Mal
Brother	Malaney
Fiance	Rohan Marley
Son	Zion
Daughter	Selah
Sign	Gemini
Hair	Dark Brown
Eyes	Brown
Nickname	L-Boogie

NEW WORDS

activist someone who is involved in supporting specific causes

audition to try out for a role

benefit concert a concert staged to raise money for a charity

chart a listing that ranks music sales

duo two people

gold record certificate awarded to a record that sells half a million (500,000) copies

gospel a type of music that celebrates Christianity

Grammy award an award given in recognition of musical achievement

hip-hop music that features breaks, multiple "samples" of songs, and often rapping

independent film a film that is made outside of Hollywood, usually with a small budget

karaoke a device that plays music while a person sings along

multicultural having or representing many different cultures

musical a play with singing and dancing

nomination selection of someone for an award

Off-Broadway a section of New York City where theaters present dramas and musicals

ovation enthusiastic applause by the audience after a performance

platinum record certificate awarded to a record that sells one million copies

producer the person who supervises the production of a film, record, or television program

R&B rhythm and blues; music that includes elements of blues and African-American folk music

rap a form of rhythmic speaking in rhyme, often spoken over a hip-hop beat

recording studio area where music is recorded and produced

refugee a person who flees to a foreign country to escape danger or abuse

reggae lively music that combines Jamaican sounds with elements of rock and blues

remix when new vocals or music are introduced so that a song sounds different

science fiction kind of story that deals with scientific subjects or alien beings

soap opera a television drama that airs in continuous episodes

solo a song or record written and performed by one
person
soul music that originated in African-American
gospel singing
trio three people

FOR FURTHER READING

George, Nelson. *Hip Hop America*. New York: Viking Press, 1998.

Nickson, Chris. *Lauryn Hill*. New York: St. Martin's Press, 1999.

Roberts, Chris. *Fugees*. London: Virgin Publishing, 1998.

Shapiro, Marc. *My Rules: The Lauryn Hill Story*. New York: The Berkley Publishing Group, 1999.

RESOURCES

WEB SITES

The Official Lauryn Hill Web site

www.lauryn-hill.com

Everything you need to know about Lauryn's music. Includes song lyrics, musical clips, tour updates, as well as personal news.

The Refugee Project

www.refugeeproject.com

This official site of Lauryn's non-profit organization details its aim and outlines the various programs. Contact information is provided to learn more about how to get involved.

INDEX

ABOUT THE AUTHOR

Cynthia Laslo was born in Norway and moved to Iowa with her parents in 1955. After high school, she taught English as a second language in the school system of Maricao, Puerto Rico.